THE LITTLE LIBRARY OF
EARTH MEDICINE

FALCON

Kenneth Meadows
Illustrations by Jo Donegan

DK PUBLISHING, INC.

A DK PUBLISHING BOOK

The Little Library of Earth Medicine was
produced, edited, and designed by
GLS Editorial and Design
Garden Studios, 11-15 Betterton Street
London WC2H 9BP

Editorial director: Jane Laing
Design director: Ruth Shane
Project designer: Luke Herriott
Editors: Claire Calman, Terry Burrows, Victoria Sorzano
US Editors: Jennifer Dorr, William Lach, Barbara Minton

Additional illustrations: Roy Flooks 16, 17, 31; John Lawrence 38
Special photography: Mark Hamilton
Picture credits: American Natural History Museum 8-9, 12, 14-15, 32

First American Edition, 1998
2 4 6 8 10 9 7 5 3 1

Published in the United States by DK Publishing, Inc.
95 Madison Avenue, New York, NY 10016
Visit us on the World Wide Web at http://www.dk.com.

Library of Congress Cataloging-in-Publication Data
Meadows, Kenneth.
    The little library of earth medicine / by Kenneth Meadows. – 1st American ed.
       p.   cm.
    Contents: |1| Falcon, 21st March-19th April – |2| Beaver, 20th April-20 May – |3|
Deer, 21st May-20th June – |4| Woodpecker, 21st June-21st July – |5| Salmon, 22nd
21st August – |6| Brown Bear, 22nd August-21st September – |7| Crow, 22nd
September-22nd October – |8| Snake, 23rd October-22nd November – |9| Owl, 23rd
November-21st December – |10| Goose, 22nd December-19 January – |11| Otter, 20th
January-18th February – |12| Wolf, 19th February-20th March.
    Includes indexes.
    ISBN 0-7894-2884-9
    1. Medicine wheels–Miscellanea. 2. Horoscopes. 3. Indians of North
America–Religion–Miscellanea. 4. Typology (Psychology)–Miscellanea. I. Title.
BF1623.M43M42 1998
133.5 9397–dc21   97-42267
                                                                                              CIP

Reproduced by Kestrel Digital Colour Ltd, Chelmsford, Essex
Printed and bound in Hong Kong by Imago

CONTENTS

INTRODUCING
EARTH MEDICINE

TO NATIVE AMERICANS, MEDICINE IS NOT AN EXTERNAL
SUBSTANCE BUT AN INNER POWER THAT IS FOUND IN
BOTH NATURE AND OURSELVES.

E arth Medicine is a unique
method of personality
profiling that draws on
Native American under-
standing of the Universe, and
on the principles embodied in
sacred Medicine Wheels.

Native Americans believed
that spirit, although invisible,
permeated Nature, so that
everything in Nature was
sacred. Animals were
perceived as acting as

messengers of spirit. They
also appeared in waking
dreams to impart power
known as "medicine." The
recipients of such dreams
honored the animal species
that appeared to them by
rendering their images on
ceremonial, ornamental,
and everyday artifacts.

NATURE WITHIN SELF

Native American shamans
– tribal wisemen –
recognized similarities
between the natural forces
prevalent during the seasons and
the characteristics of those born

Shaman's rattle
*Shamans used rattles to connect
with their inner spirit. This is a
Tlingit shaman's wooden rattle.*

*"Spirit has provided you with an opportunity to
study in Nature's university."* Stoney teaching

during corresponding times of the year. They also noted how personality is affected by the four phases of the Moon – at birth and throughout life – and by the continual alternation of energy flow, from active to passive. This view is encapsulated in Earth Medicine, which helps you to recognize how the dynamics of Nature function within you and how the potential strengths you were born with can be developed.

Animal ornament

To the Anasazi, who carved this ornament from jet, the frog symbolized adaptability.

MEDICINE WHEELS

Native American cultural traditions embrace a variety of circular symbolic images and objects. These sacred hoops have become known as Medicine Wheels, due to their similarity to the spoked wheels of the wagons that carried settlers into the heartlands of once-Native American territory. Each Medicine Wheel showed how different objects or qualities related to one another within the context of a greater whole, and how different forces and energies moved within it.

One Medicine Wheel might be regarded as the master wheel because it indicated balance within Nature and the most effective way of achieving harmony with the Universe and ourselves. It is upon this master Medicine Wheel (see pp.10–11) that Earth Medicine is structured.

Feast dish

Stylized bear carvings adorn this Tlingit feast dish. To the Native American, the bear symbolizes strength and self-sufficiency.

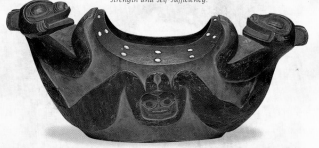

THE MEDICINE WHEEL

The outer Wheel is divided into twelve birth times, each of which has its own animal totem, and stone, tree, and color affinities.

At the hub of the Wheel, surrounded by representations of Elements, Directions, and energy flow, is the Wakan-Tanka – symbol of invisible energies coming into physical reality.

Season of birth
Each of the twelve segments relates to a specific time of year (see pp.12–13).

Wakan-Tanka
The powerful symbol used by some Native Americans to denote energy coming into form (see p.24).

NORTH: WINTER

WEST: AUTUMN

WOLF

OTTER

GOOSE

OWL

SNAKE

CROW

Stone affinity
Each birth time has a particular stone associated with it (see pp.14–15).

Tree affinity
Each birth time is connected to a type of tree (see pp.14–15).

Birth totem
An animal totem represents each birth time (see pp.16–17).

Directional totem
One of four cardinal Directions exerts an influence on each birth time (see pp.18–19).

Principal Element
Each birth time is fundamentally influenced by one of the four Elements (see pp.20–21).

Energy flow
Energy alternates between active and receptive with each birth time (see p.24).

Elemental Aspect
Each birth time has its own Elemental Aspect (see pp.20–21).

EAST: SPRING

SOUTH: SUMMER

FALCON

BEAVER

DEER

DEER

WOODPECKER

SALMON

BROWN BEAR

11

THE TWELVE
BIRTH TIMES

THE STRUCTURE OF THE MEDICINE WHEEL IS BASED
UPON THE SEASONS TO REFLECT THE POWERFUL
INFLUENCE OF NATURE ON HUMAN PERSONALITY.

The Medicine Wheel classifies human nature into twelve personality types, each corresponding to the characteristics of Nature at a particular time of the year. It is designed to act as a kind of map to help you discover your strengths and weaknesses, your inner drives and instinctive behaviors, and your true potential.

The four seasons form the basis of the Wheel's structure, with the Summer and Winter solstices and the Spring and Autumn equinoxes marking each season's passing. In Earth Medicine,

Seasonal rites

Performers at the Iroquois mid-Winter ceremony wore masks made of braided maize husks. They danced to attune themselves to energies that would ensure a good harvest.

each season is a metaphor for a stage of human growth and development. Spring is likened to infancy and the newness of life; and Summer to the exuberance of youth and of rapid development. Autumn represents the fulfillment that mature adulthood brings, while Winter symbolizes the accumulated wisdom that can be drawn upon in later life.

Each seasonal quarter of the Wheel is further divided into three periods, making twelve time segments altogether. The time of your birth determines the direction from which

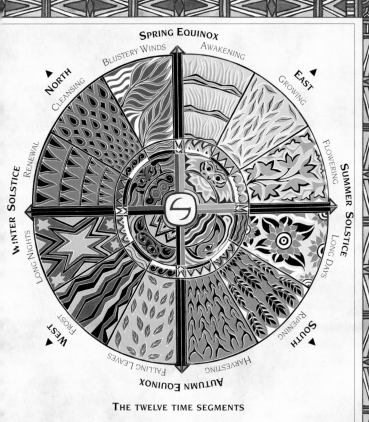

SPRING EQUINOX

BLUSTERY WINDS — AWAKENING

▲ **NORTH**

CLEANSING

RENEWAL

WINTER SOLSTICE

LONG NIGHTS

▼ **WEST**

FROST

FALLING LEAVES

AUTUMN EQUINOX

HARVESTING

RIPENING

▼ **SOUTH**

LONG DAYS

SUMMER SOLSTICE

FLOWERING

GROWING

▲ **EAST**

THE TWELVE TIME SEGMENTS

you perceive life, and the qualities imbued in Nature in that season are reflected in your core character.

Each of the twelve time segments, or birth times, is named after a feature in the natural yearly cycle. For example, the period after the Spring equinox is called Awakening time because it is the time of new growth, while the segment after the Autumn equinox is named after the falling leaves that characterize that time.

THE SIGNIFICANCE OF
TOTEMS

NATIVE AMERICANS BELIEVED THAT TOTEMS — ANIMAL
SYMBOLS — REPRESENTED ESSENTIAL TRUTHS AND ACTED
AS CONNECTIONS TO NATURAL POWERS.

A totem is an animal or natural object adopted as an emblem to typify certain distinctive qualities. Native Americans regarded animals, whose behavior is predictable, as particularly useful guides to categorizing human patterns of behavior.

A totem mirrors aspects of your nature and unlocks the intuitive knowledge that lies beyond the reasoning capacity of the intellect. It may take the form of a carving or molding, a pictorial image, or a token of fur, feather, bone, tooth, or claw. Its presence serves as an immediate link with the energies it represents. A totem is therefore more effective than a glyph or symbol as an aid to comprehending nonphysical powers and formative forces.

PRIMARY TOTEMS

In Earth Medicine you have three primary totems: a birth totem, a Directional totem, and an Elemental totem. Your *birth totem* is the embodiment of core characteristics that correspond with the dominant aspects of Nature during your birth time.

Symbol of strength

The handle of this Tlingit knife is carved with a raven and a bear head, symbols of insight and inner strength.

All twelve birth totems, each relating to a birth time, are described on pp.16–17.

Your *Directional totem* aligns you with your inner senses, which direct the main thrust of your endeavors. Each of the four seasons on the Wheel is compatible with one of the four Directions, and each of the Directions is represented by a totem. For example, Spring is associated with the East, where the sun rises, and signifies seeing things in new ways; its totem is the Eagle. The four

Prize totem

A chief or warrior of the Fox tribe affirmed his rank with this bear claw necklace.

Directional totems are explained on pp.18–19. Your *Elemental totem* relates to your instinctive behaviors. The qualities of the four Elements – Fire, Water, Earth, and Air – and their totems are introduced on pp.20–21.

THREE AFFINITIES

Each birth time also has an affinity with a tree, a stone, and a color (see pp.36–41). These three affinities have qualities that can strengthen you during challenging times.

"If a man is to succeed, he must be governed not by his inclination, but by an understanding of the ways of animals..." Teton Sioux teaching

THE TWELVE
BIRTH TOTEMS

THE TWELVE BIRTH TIMES ARE REPRESENTED BY TOTEMS,
EACH ONE AN ANIMAL THAT BEST EXPRESSES THE
QUALITIES INHERENT IN THAT BIRTH TIME.

Earth Medicine associates an animal totem with each birth time (the two sets of dates below reflect the difference in season between the Northern and Southern Hemispheres). These animals help to connect you to the powers and abilities that they represent. For an in-depth study of the Falcon birth totem, see pp.28–29.

FALCON
March 21–April 19 (N. Hem)
Sept 22–Oct 22 (S. Hem)
Falcons are full of initiative, but often rush in to make decisions they may later regret. Lively and extroverted, they have enthusiasm for new experiences but can sometimes lack persistence.

DEER
May 21–June 20 (N. Hem)
Nov 23–Dec 21 (S. Hem)
Deer are willing to sacrifice the old for the new. They loathe routine, thriving on variety and challenges. They have a wild side, often leaping from one situation or relationship into another without reflection.

BEAVER
April 20–May 20 (N. Hem)
Oct 23–Nov 22 (S. Hem)
Practical and steady, Beavers have a capacity for perseverance. Good homemakers, they are warm and affectionate but need harmony and peace to avoid becoming irritable. They have a keen aesthetic sense.

WOODPECKER
June 21–July 21 (N. Hem)
Dec 22–Jan 19 (S. Hem)
Emotional and sensitive, Woodpeckers are warm to those closest to them, and willing to sacrifice their needs for those of their loved ones. They have lively imaginations but can be worriers.

SALMON
July 22 – August 21 (N. Hem)
Jan 20 – Feb 18 (S. Hem)

Enthusiastic and self-confident, Salmon people enjoy running things. They are uncompromising and forceful, and can occasionally seem a little arrogant or self-important. They are easily hurt by neglect.

OWL
Nov 23 – Dec 21 (N. Hem)
May 21 – June 20 (S. Hem)

Owls need freedom of expression. They are lively, self-reliant, and have an eye for detail. Inquisitive and adaptable, they have a tendency to overextend themselves. Owls are often physically courageous.

BROWN BEAR
August 22 – Sept 21 (N. Hem)
Feb 19 – March 20 (S. Hem)

Brown Bears are hardworking, practical, and self-reliant. They do not like change, preferring to stick to what is familiar. They have a flair for fixing things, are good-natured, and make good friends.

GOOSE
Dec 22 – Jan 19 (N. Hem)
June 21 – July 21 (S. Hem)

Goose people are far-sighted idealists who are willing to explore the unknown. They approach life with enthusiasm, determined to fulfill their dreams. They are perfectionists, and can appear unduly serious.

CROW
Sept 22 – Oct 22 (N. Hem)
March 21 – April 19 (S. Hem)

Crows dislike solitude and feel most comfortable in company. Although usually pleasant and good-natured, they can be strongly influenced by negative atmospheres, becoming gloomy and prickly.

OTTER
Jan 20 – Feb 18 (N. Hem)
July 22 – August 21 (S. Hem)

Otters are friendly, lively, and perceptive. They feel inhibited by too many rules and regulations, which often makes them appear eccentric. They like cleanliness and order, and have original minds.

SNAKE
Oct 23 – Nov 22 (N. Hem)
April 20 – May 20 (S. Hem)

Snakes are secretive and mysterious, hiding their feelings beneath a cool exterior. Adaptable, determined, and imaginative, they are capable of bouncing back from tough situations encountered in life.

WOLF
Feb 19 – March 20 (N. Hem)
August 22 – Sept 21 (S. Hem)

Wolves are sensitive, artistic, and intuitive – people to whom others turn for help. They value freedom and their own space, and are easily affected by others. They are philosophical, trusting, and genuine.

THE INFLUENCE OF THE
DIRECTIONS

ALSO KNOWN BY NATIVE AMERICANS AS THE FOUR
WINDS, THE INFLUENCE OF THE FOUR DIRECTIONS IS
EXPERIENCED THROUGH YOUR INNER SENSES.

Regarded as the "keepers" or "caretakers" of the Universe, the four Directions or alignments were also referred to by Native Americans as the four Winds because their presence was felt rather than seen.

DIRECTIONAL TOTEMS

In Earth Medicine, each Direction or Wind is associated with a season and a time of day. Thus the three Spring birth times – Awakening time, Growing time, and Flowering time –

all fall within the East Direction, and morning. The Direction to which your birth time belongs influences the nature of your inner senses.

The East Direction is associated with illumination. Its totem is the Eagle – a bird that soars closest to the Sun and can see clearly from height. The South is the Direction of Summer and the afternoon. It signifies growth and fruition, fluidity, and emotions. Its totem, the Mouse, symbolizes productivity, feelings, and an ability to perceive detail.

"Remember...the circle of the sky, the stars, the super-natural Winds breathing night and day...the four Directions." Pawnee teaching

The four Directions

Each Direction is associated with a season and a time of day, and also with a principal function: the East with determining, the South with giving, the West with holding, and the North with receiving.

SPRING EQUINOX

NORTH

EAST

WINTER SOLSTICE

SUMMER SOLSTICE

WEST

SOUTH

AUTUMN EQUINOX

BUFFALO

EAGLE

GRIZZLY BEAR

MOUSE

The West is the Direction of Autumn and the evening. It signifies transformation – from day to night, from Summer to Winter – and the qualities of introspection and conservation. Its totem is the Grizzly Bear, which represents strength

drawn from within. The North is the Direction of Winter and the night, and is associated with the mind and its sustenance – knowledge. Its totem is the Buffalo, an animal that was honored by Native Americans as the great material "provider."

THE INFLUENCE OF THE ELEMENTS

THE FOUR ELEMENTS – AIR, FIRE, WATER, AND EARTH –
PERVADE EVERYTHING AND INDICATE THE NATURE OF
MOVEMENT AND THE ESSENCE OF WHO YOU ARE.

E lements are intangible qualities
that describe the essential state
or character of all things. In
Earth Medicine, the four Elements are
allied with four fundamental modes
of activity and are associated with
different aspects of the self. Air
expresses free movement in all
directions; it is related to the
mind and to thinking. Fire
indicates expansive
motion; it is linked with
the spirit and with
intuition. Water
signifies fluidity; it

Elemental profile
*The Elemental config-
uration of Falcon is Fire
of Fire. Fire is both the
Principal Element and
the Elemental Aspect.*

WATER

AIR

EARTH

AIR

EARTH

FIRE

has associations with the soul and the emotions. Earth symbolizes stability; it is related to the physical body and the sensations.

ELEMENTAL DISTRIBUTION

On the Medicine Wheel one Element is associated with each of the four Directions – Fire in the East, Earth in the West, Air in the North, and Water in the South. These are known as the Principal Elements.

FIRE

EARTH

FIRE

AIR

WATER

The four Elements also have an individual association with each of the twelve birth times – known as the Elemental Aspects. They follow a cyclical sequence around the Wheel based on the action of the Sun (Fire) on the Earth, producing atmosphere (Air) and condensation (Water).

The three birth times that share an Elemental Aspect belong to the same Elemental family or "clan," with a totem that gives insight into its key characteristics. Falcon people belong to the Hawk clan (see pp.34–35).

ELEMENTAL EMPHASIS

For each birth time, the qualities of the Elemental Aspect usually predominate over those of the Principal Element, although both are present to give a specific configuration, such as Fire of Earth (for Falcon's, see pp.34–35). For Falcon, Woodpecker, and Otter, the Principal Element and the Elemental Aspect are identical (for example, Air of Air), so people of these totems tend to express that Element intensely.

THE INFLUENCE OF THE MOON

THE WAXING AND WANING OF THE MOON DURING ITS
FOUR PHASES HAS A CRUCIAL INFLUENCE ON THE
FORMATION OF PERSONALITY AND HUMAN ENDEAVOR.

Native Americans regarded the Sun and Moon as indicators respectively of the active and receptive energies inherent in Nature (see p.24), as well as the measurers of time. They associated solar influences with conscious activity and the exercise of reason and the will, and lunar influences with subconscious activity and the emotional and intuitive aspects of human nature.

The Waxing Moon

This phase lasts for approximately eleven days. It is a time of growth and therefore ideal for developing new ideas and concentrating your efforts into new projects.

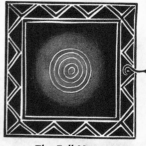

The Full Moon

Lasting about three days, this is when lunar power is at its height. It is therefore a good time for completing what was developed during the Waxing Moon.

THE FOUR PHASES

There are four phases in the twenty-nine-day lunar cycle, each one an expression of energy reflecting a particular mode of activity. They can be likened to the phases of growth of a flowering plant through the seasons: the emergence of buds (Waxing Moon), the bursting of flowers (Full Moon), the falling away of flowers (Waning Moon), and the germination of seeds (Dark Moon). The influence of each phase can be felt in two ways: in the formation of personality and in day-to-day life.

The energy expressed by the phase of the Moon at the time of your birth has a strong influence on personality. For instance, someone born during the Dark Moon is likely to be inward-looking, while a person born during the Full Moon may be more expressive. Someone born during a Waxing Moon is likely to have an outgoing nature, while a person born during a Waning Moon may be reserved. Consult a set of Moon tables to discover the phase the Moon was in on your birthday.

In your day-to-day life, the benefits of coming into harmony with the Moon's energies are considerable. Experience the energy of the four phases by consciously working with them. A Native American approach is described below.

The Waning Moon
A time for making changes, this phase lasts for an average of eleven days. Use it to improve and modify, and to dispose of what is no longer needed or wanted.

The Dark Moon
The Moon disappears from the sky for around four days. This is a time for contemplation of what has been achieved, and for germinating the seeds for the new.

THE INFLUENCE OF
ENERGY FLOW

THE MEDICINE WHEEL REFLECTS THE PERFECT BALANCE OF THE COMPLEMENTARY ACTIVE AND RECEPTIVE ENERGIES THAT COEXIST IN NATURE.

Energy flows through Nature in two complementary ways, which can be expressed in terms of active and receptive, or male and female. The active energy principle is linked with the Elements of Fire and Air, and the receptive principle with Water and Earth.

Each of the twelve birth times has an active or receptive energy related to its Elemental Aspect. Traveling around the Wheel, the two energies alternate with each birth time, resulting in an equal balance of active and receptive energies, as in Nature.

Active energy is associated with the Sun and conscious activity. Those whose birth times take this principle prefer to pursue experience. They are conceptual,

energetic, outgoing, practical, and analytical. Receptive energy is associated with the Moon and subconscious activity. Those whose birth times take this principle prefer to attract experience. They are intuitive, reflective, conserving, emotional, and nurturing.

THE WAKAN-TANKA

At the heart of the Wheel lies an S-shape within a circle, the symbol of the life-giving source of everything that comes into physical existence – seemingly out of nothing. Named by the Plains Indians as Wakan-Tanka (Great Power), it can also be perceived as energy coming into form and form reverting to energy in the unending continuity of life.

FALCON
MEDICINE

YOUR IN-DEPTH
PERSONALITY PROFILE

SEASON OF BIRTH
AWAKENING TIME

THE ENERGIZING POWER OF SPRING BURSTS FORTH
DURING THE FIRST BIRTH TIME OF THE SEASON, LENDING
THOSE BORN THEN VIGOR AND ENTHUSIASM.

Awakening time is one of the twelve birth times, the fundamental division of the year into twelve seasonal segments (see pp.12–13). As the first period of the Spring cycle, it is a time in which the Sun's energy begins to gain strength after the Winter waning, heralding one of the most rapid periods of growth in the Earth's yearly cycle.

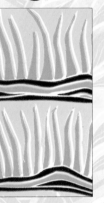

INFLUENCE OF NATURE
The qualities and characteristics imbued in Nature at this time form the basis of your own nature. So, just as Nature is springing into life again after the dormancy of Winter, if you were born during Awakening time you too have an exuberant, energetic nature, as though recently awakened refreshed and eager for action after a long rest. Your vigorous, outgoing temperament is matched by the breath of the warm, fresh Spring winds that encourage everyone out into the open after being cocooned indoors.

As new shoots emerge from the ground in a rush of new energy, so you, seeking development, go out into the world armed with ideas. The enthusiasm and confidence that accompany your desire to start new projects or to set activities in motion gives you a pioneering spirit, which means that you are often leading the way for others to follow.

STAGE OF LIFE

This time of year might be compared to the powerful urge, characteristic of childhood, to establish identity through the exercise of will.

Like a child, you have little regard for what has happened in the past or what might occur in the future. You live for the present, gaining great joy from what you are doing now. Also like a child you are impatient, with enormous amounts of energy and capability for growth. You therefore tend to have an enthusiasm for learning, which can often result in rapid self-development.

ACHIEVE YOUR POTENTIAL

The urgency inherent in your nature means that although you enter each new challenge with enthusiasm and the expectation of success, you tend to lose interest if you do not obtain quickly what you are striving for.

Nature's energy

The birth of new life is evident everywhere in this, the first cycle of Spring after the Spring equinox. Plants are in bud and there are blossoms on the trees, which also boast the first flush of green leaves.

Try to cultivate a more patient and persistent approach when seeking to realize your ideas. Like the buds that form in early Spring, your ideas are full of potential but they require careful nurturing and the co-operation of others to bring them to full maturity. Learn that adapting your ideas to suit the world does not mean that you have to compromise your principles or ideals. Listen to the advice of others; their suggestions need not diminish your ideas.

"Life is a circle from childhood to childhood; so it is with everything where power moves." Black Elk teaching

BIRTH TOTEM
THE FALCON

THE ESSENTIAL NATURE AND CHARACTERISTIC BEHAVIOR OF THE FALCON EXPRESSES THE PERSONALITY TYPE OF THOSE BORN DURING AWAKENING TIME.

Like the falcon, people born during Awakening time are energetic, enthusiastic, impulsive, and highly principled. If you were born at this time, you are likely to have an independent, passionate, and enterprising nature that thrives on constant activity and freedom from constraint.

Energetic and inquisitive, you enjoy exploring new places and ideas. Impulsive and idealistic, some of your ideas lack practicality and you tend to make hasty and ill-judged decisions. Take time to reflect on all the aspects of a situation before committing yourself to a particular course of action.

Although you enter every new project or relationship with enthusiasm, you are liable to lose interest over time, when you are particularly susceptible to distraction by something or someone new. Try to cultivate persistence and patience to ensure that you derive the fullest benefit from your endeavors and gain fulfillment from your relationships.

Independent and self-assured, you like to take the initiative at work and in your relationships. You operate well on your own and your infectious enthusiasm and pioneering spirit make you a popular and respected leader, who is always able to gain the support of others.

HEALTH MATTERS

Your drive to maintain constant
activity makes you liable to suffer
from stress, and susceptible to high
blood pressure, headaches, and
nervous disorders.
Relax and recharge
your batteries
periodically.

Falcon power

*Courageous and fast-moving, the falcon
also expresses the freedom-loving and
confident nature of the pioneering,
passionate people born at this time.*

THE FALCON AND
RELATIONSHIPS

ENTHUSIASTIC AND IMPULSIVE, FALCON PEOPLE ARE
STIMULATING FRIENDS. THEY MAKE EXCITING AND
PASSIONATE PARTNERS BUT MAY BE OVERPOSSESSIVE.

Exuberant and charismatic, Falcon people are often the leaders and initiators of their social circle. If your birth totem is Falcon, your outgoing nature tends to attract a wide group of friends. However, like your totem animal, your love of freedom and your independent streak means you dislike hangers-on, preferring the company of other self-reliant people, both socially and at work. Your frankness can sometimes upset and alienate potentially true friends, so try to curb your tactless tongue.

LOVING RELATIONSHIPS
Imaginative and prone to fantasy, Falcon people can have unrealistic expectations of their partners. Male Falcon can be a whirlwind lover, but he may also be arrogant and inconsiderate, while romantic female Falcon is often seductive but prone to bossiness. Both male and female Falcons are passionate lovers, but they can be highly possessive.

Your tendency to fly speedily into situations can land you in unsuitable relationships, and you are usually wary of commitment even with an ideal partner, so try to take things one step at a time to build intimacy.

COPING WITH FALCON
Falcon people are impulsive and love their freedom, so do not try to constrain them or they will feel stifled and threatened; give them love and approval and they will stay by choice. The best way to handle Falcon people is to share their vitality and approach them with a positive and enthusiastic attitude.

FALCON IN LOVE

Falcon with Falcon This can be an exciting and fiery match, especially if they can both learn to be less competitive and self-centered.

Falcon with Beaver Not an easy relationship. Exuberant Falcon is ill at ease with Beaver's need for security.

Falcon with Deer Falcon's enterprise suits Deer's liveliness, so this can be a sparkling pairing, but they need to stay grounded.

Falcon with Woodpecker Falcon may be attracted to Woodpecker's charm and sensuality but find such possessiveness hard to bear.

Falcon with Salmon Independent Falcon finds Salmon's bossiness annoying, but both have a warm heart to make amends.

Falcon with Brown Bear Falcon's impetuosity may not match Brown Bear's stability, but this can be an invigorating partnership.

Falcon with Crow Each can fuel the other's dreams, but Falcon's snap decisions may not suit more patient Crow.

Falcon with Snake Drawn by a magnetic attraction, both often see themselves as right, so sparks may fly.

Falcon with Owl Falcon's need for challenge matches Owl's enterprising idealism. With mutual respect, their partnership can be fulfilling.

Falcon with Goose These two have a natural affinity, but Falcon seems reckless to security-loving Goose, so there may be ups and downs.

Falcon with Otter Falcon likes doing things and Otter likes getting things done, so this can be a productive and satisfying partnership.

Falcon with Wolf Falcon's zest may seem at odds with Wolf's sensitivity, but they can work to become a well-suited couple, combining questing with caring.

DIRECTIONAL TOTEM
THE EAGLE

THE EAGLE SYMBOLIZES THE INFLUENCE OF THE EAST ON FALCON PEOPLE, WHO FOCUS ON FRESH CHALLENGES AND STRIVE FOR MENTAL AND SPIRITUAL AWARENESS.

A wakening time, Growing time, and Flowering time all fall within the quarter of the Medicine Wheel that is associated with the East Direction or Wind.

The East is aligned with Spring and the dawn of the new day, and it is therefore associated with new beginnings, openness, illumination, and revival. The power of the East's influence is primarily with the spirit, and its principal function is the power of determining. Its totem is the soaring, foresightful eagle.

The specific influence of the East on Falcon people is on open-mindedness, which brings harmony and awareness. The East Wind in

Eagle mask
This Tlingit shaman's headdress represents the eagle, which is associated with being foresightful.

this period is especially linked with new life and the enlightenment that can come to a mind unrestricted by preconceptions. It is also associated with the excitement of fresh opportunities and challenges.

EAGLE CHARACTERISTICS
The eagle can fly high in the sky, so Native Americans associated it with lofty ideals and high principles – and with illumination gained from coming closer to the spirit and the source of life. It is

The spirit of the East

The Sun rises in the East, symbolizing new beginnings; the Eagle totem signifies enlightenment and decisiveness.

also a bird that can perceive small objects from long distances, so it is associated with the ability to look ahead and take decisive action. The eagle can also soar far, wide, and high above the land, allowing it to appreciate the landscape as a whole as well as picking out details.

If your Directional totem is Eagle, you are likely to be strongly principled. You will also have an independent and adventurous spirit, which is always keen to seek out new horizons and fresh approaches. Your thinking will be toward the future, and you will have the ability to stand back from the detail and make sense of the overall pattern. In addition, your ability to see into the essence, or heart, of things will enable you to choose wisely and act firmly and decisively.

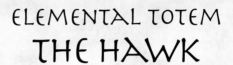

ELEMENTAL TOTEM
THE HAWK

LIKE THE HAWK, WHICH SEIZES ITS PREY AT SPEED,
FALCON PEOPLE TAKE THE INITIATIVE AND LONG FOR
THE EXCITEMENT OF A FRESH CHALLENGE.

T he Elemental Aspect of
Falcon people is Fire. They
share this Aspect with
Salmon and Owl people, who all
therefore belong to the same

Elemental family or "clan" (see
pp.20–21 for an introduction to the
influence of the Elements). Each
Elemental clan has a totem to
provide insight into its essential
qualities and characteristics.

THE HAWK CLAN

The totem of the Elemental
clan of Fire is Hawk, which
symbolizes an impulsive and
enthusiastic nature with a
pioneering spirit.

The hawk is quick
and clear-sighted,
swooping on its
prey suddenly,
seizing every opportunity.
So, if you belong to this
clan, you will have a lively
personality, are very
happy to take the lead,

Spark of vitality
The hawk symbolizes the
key qualities of Fire:
energy and enthusiasm.

and have quick and intuitive powers of understanding.

Optimistic, impulsive, and creative, you are excited by fresh ventures and fire others with the inspirational force of your enthusiasm. You dislike feeling restricted, bored, or bogged down by routine. You are often motivated by sudden flashes of inspiration, so you crave stimulation and new challenges to capture your imagination.

ELEMENTAL PROFILE

For Falcon people, the predominant Elemental Aspect of enthusiastic Fire is reinforced by your Principal Element, which is also Fire. So, if you were born at this time, you are likely to have an abundance of vitality and an energetic, intense personality, with the power to make dramatic changes around you.

You may have a tendency to lack patience and to lose interest in projects halfway through, driven by

Fire of Fire
The Element of Fire feeds Fire, generating strong enthusiasm and inspiration.

the fast-burning enthusiasm of your untempered Fire of Fire configuration. You may sometimes give up the chase before you have reached your goals, which can leave you feeling dissatisfied, frustrated, and unfulfilled.

At times like these, or when you are feeling low or overstressed, try the following revitalizing exercise. Your natural affinity with Fire means you respond well to the warming energy of the Sun, or to the air that has been cleansed by a storm. Find a quiet, open spot outside, away from the polluting effects of traffic and the activities of others.

Breathe slowly and deeply, letting the brightness of the Sun wash over you. With each in-breath, feel the energizing power of the life force bringing you inner light, recharging your body, mind, and spirit.

STONE AFFINITY
FIRE OPAL

BY USING THE GEMSTONE WITH WHICH YOUR OWN
ESSENCE RESONATES, YOU CAN TAP INTO THE POWER OF
THE EARTH ITSELF AND AWAKEN YOUR INNER STRENGTHS.

G emstones are rare minerals that are formed within the Earth itself in an exceedingly slow but continuous process. Native Americans valued gemstones not only for their beauty but also for being literally part of the Earth, and therefore possessing part of its life force. They regarded gemstones as being "alive" – channelers of energy that could be used in many ways: to heal, to protect, or to use in the practice of meditation.

Every gemstone has a different energy or vibration. On the Medicine Wheel, a stone is associated with each birth time, the energy of which

Faceted fire opal
*The fire opal is the stone of
the idealist, whose search for
truth stems from the heart
rather than the head.*

resonates with the essence of those born during that time. Because of this energy affiliation, your gemstone can be used to help bring you into harmony with the Earth and to create balance within yourself. It can enhance and develop your good qualities and endow you with the qualities or abilities you need.

ENERGY RESONANCE

Falcon people have an affinity with fire opal – a transparent, orange to red form of opal, distinct from milky-white, black, or iridescent types. Fire is the principal Element of Falcon people, and the "fire" in their stone

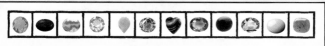

ACTIVATE YOUR GEMSTONE

O btain a fire opal and cleanse it by holding it under cold running water. Allow it to dry naturally. Then, holding the stone with both hands, bring it up to your mouth and blow into it sharply and hard, three or four times in order to impregnate it with your breath. Next, hold it firmly in one hand, and silently welcome it into your life as a friend and helper.

When you are faced with a stressful situation, use the fire opal to help you meditate on the issue and find clarity. Find a quiet spot to sit without fear of interruption, and take the fire opal in your left hand, which receives subtle energies. Focus your thoughts on the problem, and with the help of your affinity stone, seek a solution. Listen for the tranquil, quiet voice of your inner self.

represents an inner flame that produces flashes of inspiration and insight. Fire opal enhances the ability to focus and concentrate on a particular issue. Native Americans valued it for alleviating fevers and infections and for improving the eyesight – bringing outer and inner clarity.

If your birth totem is Falcon, you will find fire opal useful in resolving

Fire power
Opal is a relaxing stone that should be held to aid mental calm rather than worn all the time.

confusing and stressful situations. It adds brilliance to the intuitive senses and hones your mind's powers of reflection, making it a valuable aid when you are trying to understand changes taking place in your life.

"The outline of the stone is round; the power of the stone is endless." Lakota Sioux teaching

TREE AFFINITY
ELM

GAIN A DEEPER UNDERSTANDING OF YOUR OWN NATURE
AND AWAKEN POWERS LYING DORMANT WITHIN YOU BY
RESPECTING AND CONNECTING WITH YOUR AFFINITY TREE.

Trees have an important part to play in the protection of Nature's mechanisms and in the maintenance of the Earth's atmospheric balance, which is essential for the survival of the human race.

Native Americans referred to trees as "Standing People" because they stand firm, obtaining strength from their connection with the Earth. They therefore teach us the importance of being grounded, while at the same time listening to and reaching for our higher aspirations.

When respected as living beings, trees can provide insight into the workings of Nature and our own inner selves.

On the Medicine Wheel, each birth time is associated with a particular kind of tree, the basic qualities of which complement the nature of those born during that time. Falcon people have an affinity with the elm. This tall, stately tree has long been valued for its lumber, which is very hard and tough; it also resists the action of water, making it long-lasting and resilient.

CONNECT WITH YOUR TREE

Appreciate the beauty of your affinity tree and study its nature carefully, for it has an affinity with your own nature.

The elm is a majestic tree with ridged, dark-gray bark and serrated, bright green leaves. It grows in woods and along rivers, where it provides shade and shelter for any plants growing beneath its strong, protective branches.

Try the following exercise when you need to revitalize your inner strength. Stand beside your affinity tree. Place the palms of your hands on its trunk and rest your forehead on the backs of your hands. Inhale slowly and let energy from the tree's roots flow through your body. If easily available, obtain a cutting or twig from your affinity tree to keep as a totem or helper.

Key characteristics of the elm are durability and strength. Consequently, when enthusiasm for a project makes them impatient or blind to the needs of others, Falcon people can tap into the elm's powers of resilience and care by connecting with their tree (see panel above).

RESTORING BALANCE

If your birth totem is Falcon, you are energetic, passionate, and confident. Full of new ideas, you have a tendency to act impulsively and to make hasty judgements. This approach is often inefficient and can also make you appear selfish. The qualities of the elm can provide you with the balance you need.

When you feel that your passion for your own ideas is making you impatient or unsympathetic, call on the elm's help. Draw on its energy to replenish your own inner spirit and to enable you to reveal the compassionate side of your nature.

"All healing plants are given by Wakan-Tanka; therefore they are holy." Lakota Sioux teaching

COLOR AFFINITY
YELLOW-GREEN

ENHANCE YOUR POSITIVE QUALITIES BY USING THE
POWER OF YOUR AFFINITY COLOR TO AFFECT YOUR
EMOTIONAL AND MENTAL STATES.

ach birth time has an affinity with a particular color. This is the color that resonates best with the energies of the people born during that time, expressing their basic temperament. Exposure to your affinity color will encourage a positive emotional and mental outlook, while exposure to

colors that clash with your affinity color will have a negative effect on your sense of well-being.

Yellow-green resonates with Falcon people. Yellow is associated with the mind, stimulating new ideas and encouraging alertness. Green is the color of Nature and gradual growth. Yellow is suggestive of spontaneity, exuberance, and

Color scheme
Let a yellow-green color theme be the thread that runs through your home, from the table settings to the walls and floors.

REFLECT ON YOUR COLOR

Take two yellow and two green candles. Stand in the center of a room and position the candles around you, alternating the colors to form the corners of a large square.

Light each candle in turn to release its color energy into the atmosphere. Sit down and relax.

Enjoy the atmosphere of tranquillity in the room and focus all your attention on the two colors. Breathe slowly and rhythmically and feel your affinity color being absorbed into your body. Allow any thoughts and sensations to flow through your mind and body: experience and reflect on them.

optimism, while green indicates calmness, harmony, and balance. Yellow-green is therefore the embodiment of measured creativity, of ideas and activities channeled into purposeful development, of expansiveness balanced by calm.

COLOR BENEFITS

Strengthen your aura and enhance your positive qualities by introducing shades of yellow-green to the interior decor of your home. Spots of color can make all the difference. A yellow-green lampshade, for example, can alter the ambience of a room, or try filling a yellow-green bowl with lemons, limes, apples, and pears.

If you need a confidence boost, wear something that contains yellow-green. Whenever your energies are low, practice the color reflection exercise outlined above to balance your emotions, awaken your creativity, and help you to feel joyful.

"The power of the spirit should be honored with its color." Lakota Sioux teaching

41

WORKING THE WHEEL
LIFE PATH

CONSIDER YOUR BIRTH PROFILE AS A STARTING POINT IN
THE DEVELOPMENT OF YOUR CHARACTER AND THE
ACHIEVEMENT OF PERSONAL FULFILLMENT.

Each of the twelve birth times is associated with a particular path of learning or with a collection of lessons to be learned through life. By following your path of learning, you will develop strengths in place of weaknesses, achieve a greater sense of harmony with the world, and discover inner peace.

YOUR PATH OF LEARNING
For Falcon people, the first lesson on your path of learning is to cultivate

discernment and moderation. Your excitable temperament means that you often allow your emotions to carry you away on a tide of enthusiasm for the sparkling or new, irrespective of its true value. Next time you are presented with a glittering new project, try to rein in your emotions sufficiently in order that you can evaluate its worth with cool reason.
Consider the

"Each man's road is shown to him within his own heart. There he sees all the truths of life." Cheyenne teaching

negative aspects as well as the positive before deciding whether to commit your considerable energies to its development.

Falcon people also need to develop patience and perseverance. Starting a new project or leading a new venture comes easily to you, but you often lose interest well before the project is finished. Try to maintain your enthusiasm to the end of a project by breaking it down into a series of smaller tasks or milestones, and by focusing your energy on achieving each step of your journey in turn.

Your third lesson is to cultivate a more cautious and less trusting attitude toward others. Some people have a tendency to take advantage of your enthusiastic desire to help them, and will try to manipulate you to their own ends. Before you leap to their assistance, analyze their motives and make sure you are being true to your own principles.

WORKING THE WHEEL
MEDICINE POWER

HARNESS THE POWERS OF OTHER BIRTH TIMES TO
TRANSFORM YOUR WEAKNESSES INTO STRENGTHS AND
TO MEET THE CHALLENGES IN YOUR LIFE.

he whole spectrum of human qualities and abilities is represented on the Medicine Wheel. The totems and affinities associated with each birth time indicate the basic qualities with which those born at that time are equipped.

Complementary affinity
A key strength of Crow – weak in Falcon – is the ability to act with patience and tact.

Study your path of learning (see pp.42–43) to identify aspects of your personality that may need to be strengthened, then look at other birth times to discover the totems and affinities that can assist you in this task. For example, your Elemental profile is Fire of Fire (see pp.34–35), so for balance you need the stabilizing qualities of Earth, the

freedom of Air, and the adaptive nature of Water. Brown Bear's Elemental profile is Earth of Water, Snake's is Water of Earth, and Otter's is Air of Air, so meditate on these birth totems. In addition, you may find it useful to study the profiles of the other two members of your Elemental clan of Hawk – Salmon and Owl – to discover how the same Elemental Aspect can be expressed differently.

Also helpful is the birth totem opposite yours on the Wheel, which contains qualities that complement or enhance your own. This is known as your complementary affinity, which for Falcon people is Crow.

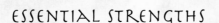

ESSENTIAL STRENGTHS

Described below are the essential strengths of each birth totem. To develop a quality that is weak in yourself or that you need to meet a particular challenge, meditate upon the birth totem that contains the attribute you need. Obtain a representation of the relevant totem – a claw, tooth, or feather; a picture, ring, or model. Affirm that the power it represents is within you.

Falcon medicine is the power of keen observation and the ability to act decisively and energetically whenever action is required.

Beaver medicine is the ability to think creatively and laterally – to develop alternative ways of doing or thinking about things.

Deer medicine is characterized by sensitivity to the intentions of others and to that which might be detrimental to your well-being.

Woodpecker medicine is the ability to establish a steady rhythm throughout life and to be tenacious in protecting all that you value.

Salmon medicine is the strength to be determined and courageous in the choice of goals you want to achieve and to have enough stamina to see a task through to the end.

Brown Bear medicine is the ability to be resourceful, hardworking, and dependable in times of need, and to draw on inner strength.

Crow medicine is the ability to transform negative or nonproductive situations into positive ones and to transcend limitations.

Snake medicine is the talent to adapt easily to changes in circumstances and to manage transitional phases well.

Owl medicine is the power to see clearly during times of uncertainty and to conduct life consistently, according to long-term plans.

Goose medicine is the courage to do whatever might be necessary to protect your ideals and to adhere to your principles in life.

Otter medicine is the ability to connect with your inner child, to be innovative and idealistic, and to thoroughly enjoy the ordinary tasks and routines of everyday life.

Wolf medicine is the courage to act according to your intuition and instincts rather than your intellect, and to be compassionate.